The Great Adventure Baker

JANE DIXON-SMITH

Dedicated to my mum, Mollie Dixon,
who loved to bake.

(1955 - 2022)

Contents

Foreword

Baking has always been a huge passion of mine. When I was little, Mum baked many scones, fairy cakes and flans on weekend mornings in the tiny kitchen of the first home I remember. Afterwards, Mum would always let us lick the spoon.

She was an avid baker and was regularly commissioned to make celebration cakes for other people. She also did her utmost to fulfil my and my siblings' demands for our dream birthday cake each year. (The black food colouring for the Batman cake took a long time to fade on her hands!) Playgroups and schools could always rely on her to provide a glut of tasty treats for fundraisers too.

Later, she would run a tearoom, together with my youngest brother, and a stall at various agricultural shows, markets, and fairs throughout the year.

One of the biggest complaints she always made at funerals would be the lack of cake – specifically a proper fruit cake. "People have travelled far," she would say, "the least you can do is provide them with a decent slice of cake for afters."

Most years she would make a number of Christmas cakes and hand them out. When she died suddenly at the beginning of 2022, I still had the one she had made me the Christmas before.

We served that fruitcake, the one she herself had made, at her funeral tea. She would have loved that.

My own passion for baking has never reached beyond laying on a spread for friends and family, school fundraisers, and taking a box of brownies or other goodies to share on mountain walks.

I bake often with my children, particularly William, who has declared that he definitely wants to be a baker when he grows up.

I spend an awful lot of my spare time outdoors in the Lake District where I live, venturing into Wales to scramble and climb, heading off into the Scottish wilderness to summit some of the Highland's mountains, conquering 4000m peaks in the Swiss Alps, and camping in the arctic wilderness on Svalbard.

Sometimes I think my active lifestyle is a necessity to combat all the cake I eat, but it does fuel the body and provide a much-needed boost, particularly for my least favourite bit – the uphill parts.

In this book I share my favourite recipes for bakes I take with me on my adventures, from the staple chocolate brownie and protein packed granola bars, to a couple of savoury recipes I find work really well on the go. I've always shared my recipes with everyone who has asked me, so it seemed only fitting I should put together a concise edition of all the ones I have loved making over the years.

I hope you enjoy!

Jane Dixon-Smith

Sweet
Bakes

Grasmere Gingerbread

In the heart of the Lake District is a little village called Grasmere, and in the middle of that little village is an even littler shop. The world-renowned Grasmere Gingerbread Shop was once home to Sarah Nelson, the Victorian cook who created the chewy gingerbread back in 1854.

The exact recipe is well-kept secret, but this version works a little better I think for the cold mountains in winter, as it's not quite as hard as the shop-bought variety.

Ingredients

180oz diced cold butter

230g plain flour

½ tsp bicarbonate of soda

½ tsp cream of tartar

3 tsp ground ginger (or 2 tsp if you prefer slightly less ginger)

180g soft light brown sugar

1 tbsp golden syrup

Demerara sugar

Method

1. Preheat the oven to 150C fan.

2. Place the butter, flour, bicarbonate of soda, cream of tartar and ground ginger in a bowl. I use 3 teaspoons of ginger because I like it to really have a kick, but if you prefer, use 2. Rub the ingredients together until you have a fine breadcrumb consistency.

3. Rub in the sugar, again with your fingertips. The mixture can be a little sticky if it's warm in the kitchen, but don't worry.

4. Finally, gently and quickly rub in the golden syrup. You can stir this in with a round bladed-knife until it's fairly evenly distributed if you prefer.

5. Place the mixture into a lined 17.5 x 27.5cm deep rectangle tin and bake for around 30 minutes until just golden on top.

6. When taking the cake out on the mountains, I find it can be a little too hard in the cold weather, so baking it for only 30 minutes you get a softer, more chewy consistency than if you baked it for 40-45 minutes, when it can be a little more biscuit-like.

7. Finally, sprinkle the gingerbread with demerara sugar whilst hot and leave to cool.

Light Gingerbread

This lighter gingerbread recipe is beautifully moist and if you can bear to leave it for a day or two in an airtight container it develops a rich, sticky top. I add more ginger and cinnamon to mine as I like the spicy flavours, but you can use less if you wish. It's a really warming cake for a cold day, and goes well with a flask of coffee.

Ingredients

140g dried pitted whole dates

75ml rapeseed oil

75g black treacle

50g maple syrup

2 tsp freshly grated ginger

1 large egg

175ml whole milk

250g plain flour

1 tsp bicarbonate of soda

1 tsp ground ginger

1 tsp cinnamon

50g dark muscovado sugar

Method

1. First, place the dates into a bowl and cover with 125ml of boiling water.

2. Line a 17.5 x 27.5cm deep rectangle tin with baking parchment.

3. Put the oil, treacle, maple syrup, fresh ginger, egg and milk in a small bowl and mix together.

4. In a separate large bowl mix the flour, bicarbonate of soda, ground ginger, cinnamon and sugar.

5. Heat the oven to 140C fan.

6. Blend the date mixture with a small food processor or hand blender to make a thick puree.

7. Pour all the wet ingredients into the bowl with the dry ingredients and mix everything together until combined into a batter-like consistency.

8. Pour the mixture into the lined tin and bake in the oven for 40-45 minutes, until a knife or skewer inserted into the centre comes out clean.

9. Cool on a wire rack.

10. Once completely cold, place in an airtight container or wrap in parchment and then tightly with foil. The cake will be sticky when left for a day and the flavours richer.

Pistachio, Courgette and Lemon Cake

I absolutely adore this squishy, lemony cake. You'd never really know courgette was such a big player here, as it's not really that noticeable as such, but it adds a fantastic texture and moistness to the sponge, a little similar to carrot cake.

Ingredients

180g shelled pistachios

250g golden caster sugar

200g softened butter

280g plain flour

1 ¼ tsp baking powder

1 ¼ tsp bicarbonate

3 large eggs

140g full fat plain yoghurt (I use Greek)

3 lemons, zest and juice

140g coarsely grated courgette

180g icing sugar

Method

1. Heat the oven to 160C fan and line a 17.5 x 27.5cm deep rectangular tin with baking parchment.

2. Grind most of pistachios in a small food processor, reserving a handful for decoration, or alternatively finely chop.

3. Cream the butter and sugar together until soft and fluffy.

4. Add the ground pistachios, flour, baking powder, bicarbonate of soda, eggs, yoghurt, zest of three lemons and juice of two lemons. Beat with an electric whisk until well combined.

5. Fold in the courgette and then place the mixture into the lined tin.

6. Bake for 35-40 minutes until a skewer inserted into the centre comes out clean.

7. Leave to cool on a wire rack. Once completely cold, remove from the tin and peel off the baking parchment.

8. Mix the icing sugar with the remaining lemon juice until you have a thick, runny consistency. Drizzle over the top of the cake and sprinkle with the remaining pistachios for decoration.

Empire Biscuits

These delightful biscuits are a firm favourite with my children, who love sandwiching them together and adding the icing and cherries. They're popular in Scotland and Northern Ireland, as well as other Commonwealth countries. I last ate them on the top of Ben Vorlich.

Ingredients

300g plain flour

200g salted butter

100g caster sugar

1 large egg

Raspberry jam

100g icing sugar

Glacé cherries

Method

1. Preheat the oven to 160C fan. Beat the butter and sugar until creamed together.

2. Add the flour and egg and mix with a round-bladed knife until the mixture starts coming together, then form into a ball of dough with your hands. Rest for 30 minutes in the fridge if time allows.

3. Cut the dough in half and roll out each ball in turn onto a lightly floured surface to approximately 5mm thick.

4. Use a fluted cutter to cut out an even number of biscuits and place onto a lined baking sheet.

5. Bake for around 10 - 12 minutes, until just starting to turn golden brown.

6. Once your biscuits are cool, spread a small teaspoon of jam over half the biscuits and then sandwich the other half of biscuits on top.

7. Mix the icing sugar with a very small amount of water to create a thick, spreadable icing, and use a teaspoon to coat a small amount onto the top of each biscuit.

8. Add half a glacé cherry to the top of each and you're done!

Rhubarb and Custard Cake

I first made this cake after receiving a glut of rhubarb from my dad's garden. It's tangy, stodgy, and absolutely delicious. I make it in the summer with freshly cut rhubarb and serve it warm with ice cream, and in the winter using rhubarb frozen from the previous summer months, served with custard. At both times of year I wrapped what was left in a kitchen towel placed in a small container to take out on the mountains.

Ingredients

400g rhubarb

50g caster sugar

250g butter

250g golden caster sugar

150g custard

250g self-raising flour

½ tsp baking powder

4 large eggs

1 tsp vanilla extract

Method

1. Place the rhubarb in a roasting tin, sprinkle with 50g of caster sugar and bake for 15 minutes on 180C fan. Leave the oven on ready for baking the cake. Carefully drain the juice from the tray and leave to cool.

2. Beat the butter and sugar together until light and fluffy. Add the self-raising flour, baking powder, eggs and vanilla extract and beat again until combined. Fold in the roasted rhubarb.

3. Place in a lined 17.5 x 27.5cm deep rectangle tin and bake in the preheated oven for 55 minutes. Check at 50 minutes. It may need 5 minutes more. The cake is done when a knife or skewer inserted into the centre comes out clean.

4. Place the tray on a wire rack until it is cool enough to remove the cake, then place back on the wire rack until completely cold.

Berry and Seed Granola Bars

I first made these granola bars as a quick, high-energy fix for eating on the go. They proved very effective when munched quickly at the car as we booted-up and got our kit together before tackling Scottish mountains. You can mix and match the ingredients easily enough if you prefer other seeds or nuts.

Ingredients

100g butter

3 tbsp honey

100g light muscovado sugar

200g porridge oats

100g cranberries

100g sunflower seeds

50g sesame seeds

50g cashew nuts

1 tsp cinnamon

Method

1. Heat the oven to 160C fan. Butter and line a 17.5 x 27.5cm rectangular tin with baking parchment.

2. Warm the butter, honey and sugar gently in a pan until just melted.

3. Add in the oats, fruit, nuts and cinnamon and stir until well combined.

4. Tip the mixture into the tin and press down lightly with the back of a spoon or spatula.

5. Bake for 30 minutes.

6. Once cool, cut into bars and wrap in greaseproof paper.

Welsh Cakes

I've made these a number of times to take into the Welsh mountains when out climbing and walking. I love how easy they are to make, being one of the few sweet treats you fry instead of baking.

Ingredients

270g plain flour

1 ½ tsp baking powder

½ tsp cinnamon

½ tsp mixed spice

Pinch of nutmeg

130g cold butter, diced

90g caster sugar

70g currants

1 medium egg

1-3 tbsp whole milk

Method

1. Sift the flour, baking powder and spices into a mixing bowl. Rub in the butter and sugar with your fingertips until it resembles fine breadcrumbs.

2. Stir in the currants, then mix in the egg. Bring together with a round-bladed knife, adding a little milk if needed, and finally bring together into a ball of dough with your hands.

3. Roll out the dough on a lightly floured surface until about 5mm thick. Using a 7.5cm fluted cutter stamp out the cakes. Reroll any remnants and repeat.

4. Heat a heavy-based, flat-bottom frying pan over a low heat.

5. Once hot, place the Welsh cakes into the pan in batches, cooking for a few minutes on each side until they are golden brown.

6. Sprinkle with a little extra caster sugar to finish.

Bonfire Toffee

A firm favourite amongst many of my friends and family, this delicious, treacly toffee can be put in a zip-lock bag and stuffed in your rucksack for any adventure.

Ingredients

75g golden syrup

75g black treacle

150g light soft brown sugar

75g butter

¼ tsp cream of tartar

Method

1. Line a 17.5 x 27.5cm tin with baking parchment.

2. Place all the ingredients into a heavy-based pan over a medium heat. Use a confectionary thermometer. It is best to put this in the pan at the start, so that it heats along with the ingredients, to avoid damage to the thermometer.

3. Stir occasionally until the butter is melted and sugar dissolved.

4. Increase the heat and bring the mixture to the boil. Take off the heat once it reaches 140C/285F. It can take a while, but you need to wait until it just reaches temperature.

5. Pour the mixture carefully into the lined tin, making sure not to splash yourself with the boiling mixture.

6. Once the toffee has cooled enough to handle, mark the surface as deeply as you can with a sharp knife. Then once cooled completely you should be able to break the toffee into even pieces.

7. Store in an airtight container.

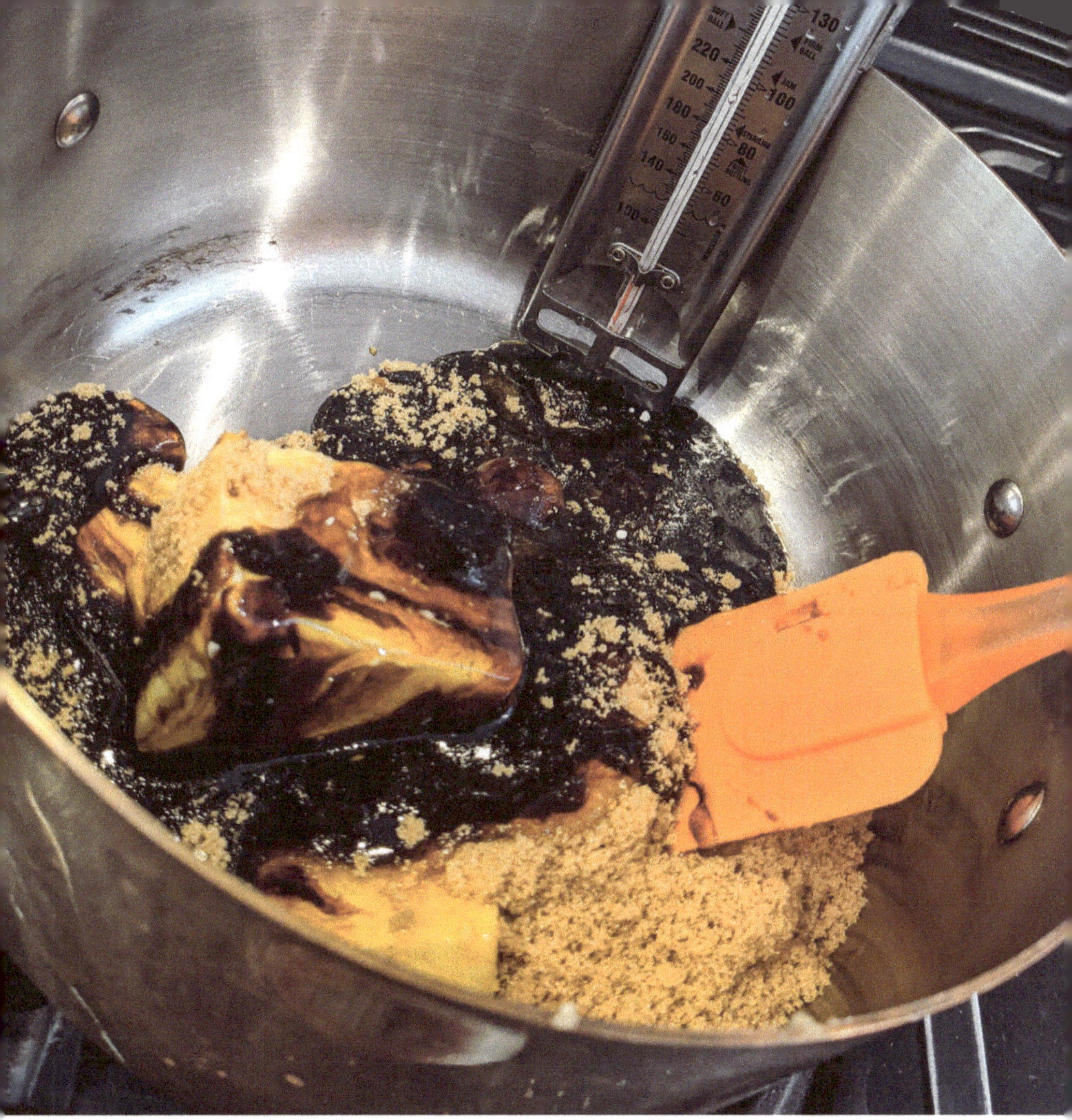
130
220
200
100
180
160
80
140
60
100

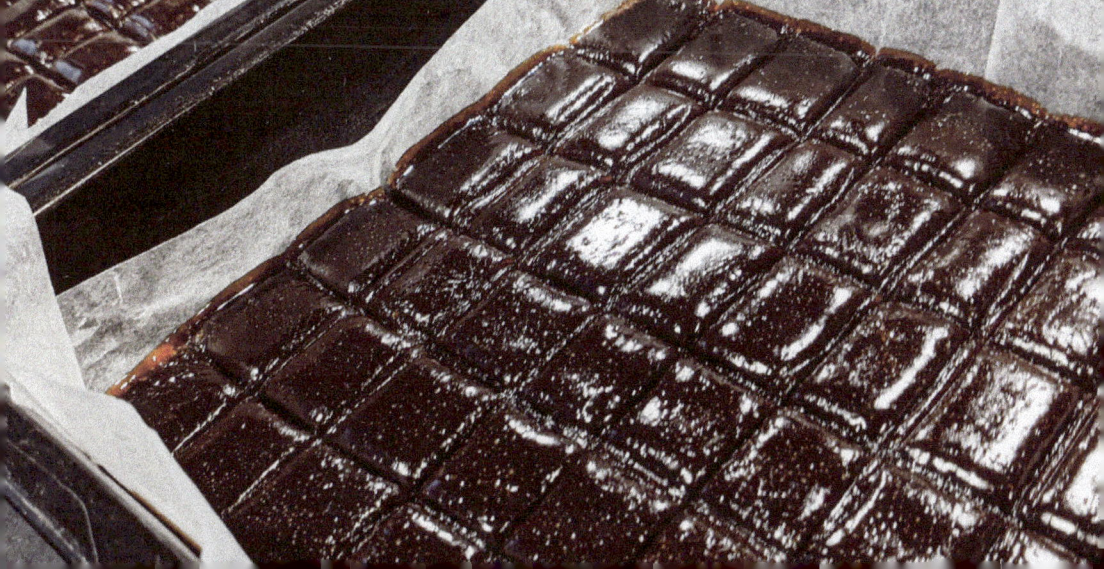

Ginger Crunch

It's true, I'm a big fan of ginger. Even in the summer months the hills and mountains can be cold places, and I think gingery bakes give you a little extra warmth. And I love the flavour.

The fudge topping of this particular bake works really well with the crunchy biscuit base.

Ingredients

For the base:

140g plain flour

60g caster sugar

½ tsp baking powder

1 tsp ground ginger

90g cold butter diced

For the topping:

90g butter

50g golden syrup

190g icing sugar

1 tsp ground ginger

Method

1. Heat the oven to 160C fan and line a 17.5 x 27.5cm deep rectangle tin with baking parchment.

2. For the shortbread base, place the flour, sugar, baking powder, ginger and butter in a large mixing bowl and rub together until you have a fine breadcrumb consistency.

3. Place the shortbread mixture into your tin and press firmly down using the back of a spoon.

4. Bake for 15-20 minutes until golden brown and then cool on a wire rack. Turn off the oven.

5. Whilst the shortbread cools, you can make the fudge topping.

6. Place the butter and syrup in a pan and melt over a low heat.

7. Take off the heat and sift the icing sugar and ginger into the butter mixture and beat with an electric hand mixer until smooth. This should take around 2 minutes.

8. Spread the topping over the shortbread base and leave to set before cutting into bars. You can chill in the fridge to speed this along.

Flapjack

A staple food for everyone's rucksack, these flapjacks are great emergency supplies when we're out walking in the picturesque villages near home and 4000m Alpine peaks alike. For years I made a Delia Smith recipe which I absolutely loved for its chewy, toffee-like texture. But in cold climates it was often hard to bite into. This one is a bit softer and I've added additional fruits.

Ingredients

175g butter

175g soft brown sugar

1 tbsp golden syrup

250g porridge oats

Plus of any of the following:

50g chopped apricots

50g sultanas and 1 tsp cinnamon

50g chopped dates and 1 tsp mixed spice

Zest of one lemon (drizzle the top of the flapjack with some white chocolate once cool)

Method

1. Preheat the oven to 150C fan. Line a 20cm square tin.

2. In a large pan, heat the butter, sugar and golden syrup over a low heat until melted.

3. Remove from the heat and stir in the porridge oats and any other ingredients you choose to add to your flapjack.

4. Spoon into your tin and level using the back of a spatula. Bake for 20 minutes or until the edges are brown and golden.

5. Place the tin on a wire rack and wait until completely cool before removing and cutting into squares.

6. Drizzle with melted chocolate if you like.

Ginger Fruit Cake

I've taken this out on group walks many times, and it's always a big hit, even with those who aren't normally partial to fruit cake. It's deeply rich in flavour, and has a beautiful aroma from the Cointreau. I usually make this as my Christmas cake each year as it's by far one of my favourite fruit cake recipes. The best part is there's no need to soak the fruit the day before.

Ingredients

225g sultanas

225g raisins

330g figs, chopped

330g prunes, chopped

300g crystalised ginger

150g stem ginger from a jar, chopped

3 tbsp stem ginger syrup from the jar above

6 tbsp Cointreau

2 tsp ginger

2 tsp mixed spice

Zest of 3 lemons

225ml olive oil

260g light muscovado sugar

6 eggs

340g plain flour

1 ½ tsp baking powder

Method

1. Heat the oven to 120C fan. Line a 20cm, very deep, square cake tin with baking parchment.

2. Mix the dried fruits, ginger, syrup, Cointreau, spices and lemon zest together and set aside.

3. In a large mixing bowl, whisk the olive oil, sugar and eggs together with an electric whisk until light and fluffy.

4. Sift the flour and baking powder into the mixture, add the fruit, and fold everything together until thoroughly combined.

5. Spoon the mixture into the cake tin. Then wrap the entire cake tin in another layer of baking parchment to avoid burning the cake. Bake for around 3-4 hours until a skewer inserted into the centre comes out clean (my oven bakes this cake in 3 hours 30 minutes, but I'd check after 3 hours).

6. Cool on a wire rack. Once cold, wrap tightly in baking parchment and then tinfoil.

7. I make this cake well ahead of when I intend to eat it, as it's best left for a few weeks for all the beautiful fruits to mature in the cake. You can also feed the cake with a couple of extra tablespoons of Cointreau immediately after baking, then again a few weeks later.

You can make this cake in a traditional round tin if you prefer. Simply use two-thirds of the ingredients in the recipe and check the cake after 2 hours 30 minutes.

Mince Pies

My children love making mince pies with me every year. They're a firm favourite both straight out of the oven with a spot of cream or ice cream, and likewise they make a great sharing snack when out and about.

Ingredients

450g plain flour

250g packet of cold, block butter

60g lard

60g caster sugar

2 egg yolks

5 tbsp cold water

Method

1. Weigh out the flour, butter and lard in a large bowl. Using a cheese grater, grate the butter and lard into the flour. Keep dipping the block of butter into the flour if it gets a bit sticky.

2. Add the sugar and egg yolks (you can freeze the whites to use for meringue at a later date) and rub in with your fingertips.

3. Add the water a little at a time and stir together with a round-bladed knife, and finally bring the mixture together into a ball of dough with your hands. Refrigerate for 30 mins.

4. Heat the oven to 180C fan and place three, 12-hole, shallow muffin tins in to preheat.

5. Divide the pastry into two and roll out until around 3mm thick. Cut out an even number of rounds for your pie bottoms and lids. I use an 8cm cutter for the bottoms and a 6.5cm cutter for the lids. You want the lids to be the same size as the holes of your bun tin, and the bottoms to be a little larger so they come up the sides.

6. Take the pre-heated baking tins from the oven and carefully line the bottom of each muffin hole with a larger round. Put a teaspoon of mincemeat in the centre of each, careful not to overfill otherwise they leak out during cooking and stick to the tin. Then place a lid snugly on top of each one.

7. Prick the top of each lid with a fork and bake in the oven for 20 minutes until golden brown. Dust with icing sugar.

Homemade Mincemeat

I always make my own mincemeat in my slow cooker. I think the ingredients really pack flavour when they've been simmered for a while then jarred a few months in advance of the festive season. Plus your whole house will smell amazing!

I far prefer using butter to suet for a beautiful rich flavour, and it's also suitable for vegetarians. I've never been a huge fan of currants so I use a lot of raisins and sultanas instead, but you can play about with the ratios to your liking.

Ingredients

350g raisins

350g sultanas

Zest of one orange

Zest and juice of one lemon

2 small apples, peeled, cored and finely chopped

125g butter

225g light muscovado sugar

1 tsp ground cinnamon

2 tsp mixed spice

200ml brandy or rum

Method

Place all the ingredients in a slow cooker and leave on low for around 3 hours. Alternatively place everything in a large pan and simmer for 20 minutes. Spoon into four 370g sterile jars and secure the lids. Store in a cool place out of direct sunlight for up to 12 months.

Chewy Chocolate Orange Brownies

I originally acquired this recipe from the owner of a café in Windermere over fifteen years ago. I bought a slice often, and when I discovered the café was going to close down, I asked for a copy and the owner generously shared it with me. I've added orange zest and tweaked the timings for a fan oven. It's great for taking out on a hot day when you want chocolate without the risk of it making a melted mess.

Ingredients

100g butter

100g plain chocolate

300g caster sugar

2 tsp vanilla extract

Zest of three oranges (you can use two but I always like to make a punch with the flavour), or 50g of your favourite chopped nuts

2 large eggs

100g plain flour

2 tbsp cocoa powder

Method

1. Preheat the oven to 160C fan. Line a 20cm square tin with baking parchment.

2. Melt the butter and chocolate in a glass mixing bowl over a pan of simmering water. Remove from the heat and allow to cool slightly.

3. Pour the sugar, vanilla and orange zest into the melted ingredients and beat well with a wooden spoon.

4. Add the eggs one at a time, beating between each addition.

5. Sift in the flour and cocoa powder and mix well until you have a smooth, thick batter.

6. Spoon into the baking tin and bake for 25-30 minutes until a skewer inserted into the centre comes out clean.

Carrot Cake

I love this light carrot cake recipe. I'm allergic to certain nuts and as carrot cake often contains the likes of walnuts, I steer clear unless I've made it myself. I also like the zesty icing, rather than a thick layer of buttercream. It's a real delight on a sunny day with a glass of lemonade.

Ingredients

175g light muscovado sugar

175ml sunflower oil

3 large eggs

140g grated carrot (roughly 3 medium carrots)

100g sultanas

Zest of 1 large orange (or 2 if you want to use one to decorate)

175g self-raising flour

1 tsp bicarbonate of soda

1 tsp ground cinnamon

½ tsp freshly grated nutmeg (or ground is fine too)

175g icing sugar

1-2 tbsp orange juice

Method

1. Preheat the oven to 160C fan. Line a 20cm square cake tin with baking parchment.

2. Place the sugar, sunflower oil and eggs in a large mixing bowl and mix well, ensuring there are no lumps of sugar.

3. Add the carrots, sultanas and orange zest.

4. Sift the flour, bicarbonate of soda and spices into the bowl and lightly mix with a wooden spoon until the ingredients are combined. You should have a runny, batter-like consistency.

5. Pour the mixture into the lined tin and bake for 40-45 minutes until a skewer inserted into the centre of the cake comes out clean.

6. Cool on a wire rack.

7. Once completely cold, mix the icing sugar with the orange juice until you have a thick, runny icing, and drizzle across the top of the cake. I use the zest of a second orange to decorate the top.

8. Store in an airtight container.

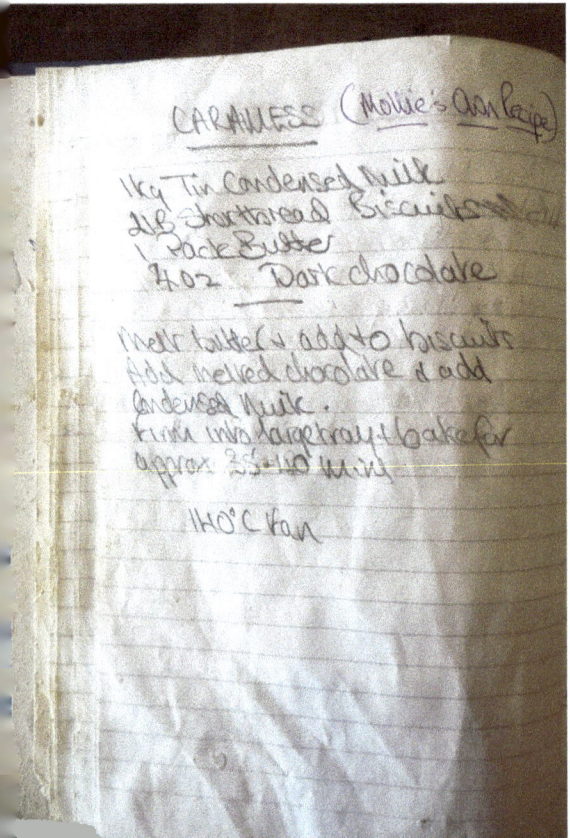

CARAMESS (Mollie's Own Recipe)

1kg Tin Condensed Milk
2lb Shortbread Biscuits
1 Pack Butter
4oz Dark chocolate

Melt butter & add to biscuits
Add melted chocolate & add
condensed Milk.
turn into large tray + bake for
approx 35 + 40 mins

140°C Fan

My mum's invention, Caramess, is really easy to make, a proper doorstopper of a cake – especially if you make it on her industrial scale of more than 2-kilogram batches.

Mollie's Caramess

My mum was awfully proud of this invention. It came about after she made a mess of a millionaire's shortbread recipe when attempting to scale it up to sell at a farmer's market. She didn't want to waste the ingredients and decided to mix it all together, bake it, and thus she birthed her signature bake ... Caramess!

For this recipe I have downscaled her original. I've also standardised the ingredients to grams rather than the combination of grams and ounces. Who knew you could buy 1kg tins of condensed milk? Yes, you can!

Ingredients

397g tin of condensed milk

400g shortbread biscuits

100g butter

50g dark chocolate

Method

1. Preheat the oven to 140C fan. Line a 17.5 x 27.5cm deep rectangle tin with baking parchment.

2. Melt butter and chocolate together in a large pan over a low heat, or in a bowl over a pan of simmering water. Once completely melted remove from the heat.

3. Meanwhile, roughly chop the shortbread biscuits into small pieces.

4. Tip the shortbread and the condensed milk into the melted ingredients and fold together thoroughly.

5. Press down into the lined baking tin and bake for approximately 35-40 minutes.

6. Leave to completely cool before cutting into squares.

7. The biscuit pieces should stay crunchy if you store in an airtight container.

Funfetti Cake

With a heavy dose of hundreds and thousands, this cake is great for kids to make and take with them on adventures.

Ingredients

350g self-raising flour

175g caster sugar

175g butter

120ml whole milk

3 large eggs

200g icing sugar

Sprinkles (lots!)

Method

1. Preheat the oven to 150C. Line a 17.5 x 27.5cm deep rectangle tin with baking parchment.

2. Melt the butter in a small saucepan over a low heat. Meanwhile, combine the flour and sugar in a large mixing bowl.

3. Pour the melted butter and eggs into the dry ingredients and beat well until fully combined.

4. Add the milk and stir again before pouring in to the prepared cake tin.

5. Bake for 35 minutes until a skewer inserted into the centre of the cake comes out clean.

6. Cool on a wire rack until completely cold before mixing the icing sugar with a little water or lemon juice until you have a thick, runny consistency, and spread evenly over the top of the cake.

7. Decorate with sprinkles. Lots of them. And kids, don't forget to get as many on the floor as on the cake!

Mum's Banana Bread

I've always been fond of banana bread and it's a great way to use up overripe bananas.

I thought I had a great recipe, until my mum shared this one with me. She used to bake it all the time and everyone devoured it, especially warm. Then I discovered my children were deliberately avoiding eating the bananas in the fruit bowl hoping I would eventually use them up and bake a banana bread.

Ingredients

3 medium bananas

110g butter

110g demerara sugar

110g caster sugar

1 egg

275g self-raising flour

1 tsp baking powder

1 tsp vanilla extract

Method

1. Preheat the oven to 170C fan. Line a 2lb loaf tin with baking parchment.

2. Melt the butter in a small saucepan over a low heat.

3. Break the bananas into chunks in a large mixing bowl. Add all the ingredients, including the butter.

4. Mix with an electric hand whisk until thoroughly combined.

5. Pour into the pre-lined loaf tin and bake for around 1-1 ¼ hours, until a skewer inserted into the centre comes out clean.

6. If left to cool and stored overnight in an airtight container the top will go a lovely sticky texture. Alas this hardly ever happens in my house as it's usually all gone within an hour of coming out of the oven.

This is the original recipe my mum wrote down for me many years ago and which I've used for my banana bread ever since. I'm not sure I ever did tell her it was far better than the recipe I had already.

Banana Bread
___

3 Medium Bananas
4oz Melted Butter
8oz Dem sugar d Caster 4oz
4oz Together
1 Egg
10 oz Flour (Self Raising
1 tspn B. Powder
vanilla Extract

Lemon and Poppyseed Cake

The yoghurt in this recipe gives it a lovely, moist texture. It has a heavy, pudding-like consistency, which I love. And baking it in a square tin instead of a deep loaf tin means you can cut it into nine neat squares with more surface area for icing!

Ingredients

175g softened butter

175g golden caster sugar

200g self-raising flour

Zest of 4 lemons

3 eggs

2 tbsp poppy seeds

125g natural yoghurt

200g icing sugar

Juice of 2 lemons

Method

1. Preheat the oven to 160C fan. Line a 20cm square tin with baking parchment.

2. Beat the butter and sugar together in a large mixing bowl until light and fluffy.

3. Add all the other ingredients and beat again until well combined.

4. Put the mixture into the pre-lined baking tin and level with the back of the spoon or spatula. Bake in the oven for 40-45 minutes until a skewer inserted into the centre comes out clean.

5. Cool on a wire rack. Once completely cold, mix the icing sugar with the lemon juice until you have a thick, runny consistency, and drizzle over the top of the cake and leave until set.

There's only one downside to this cake, and that is finding poppyseeds in your teeth for hours later, but it's worth it.

Rosemary Shortbread

I'd never thought of adding rosemary to shortbread before my mum gave me this recipe. You can also substitute the rosemary for the same quantity of lavender flowers, but rosemary is my favourite. You can also add the zest of a lemon for a note of citrus. The addition of semolina gives it a nice little crunch.

Ingredients

225g plain flour

100g semolina

225g butter

100g caster sugar

2 tbsp freshly chopped rosemary

Method

1. Preheat the oven to 140C fan. Line a 20cm x 20cm tin with baking parchment.

2. Place all the ingredients into a bowl and rub together with your fingertips. Be patient, it will take a while, but eventually it will start to come together into a dough.

3. Press the dough down into the bottom of the cake tin evenly. Mark the surface into fingers with a knife, and prick all over with a fork.

4. Chill in the fridge for 30 minutes.

5. Bake for 35 minutes until pale, golden brown. Cool on a wire rack before cutting along the scored lines.

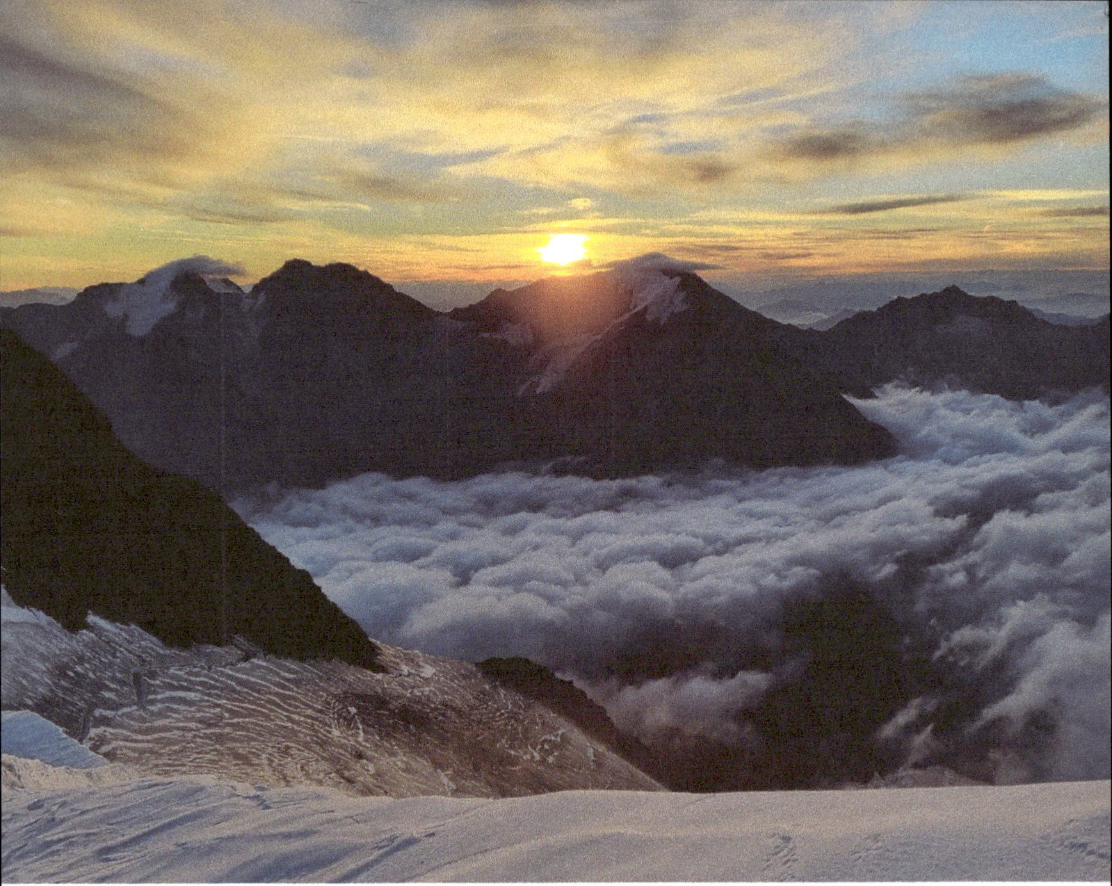

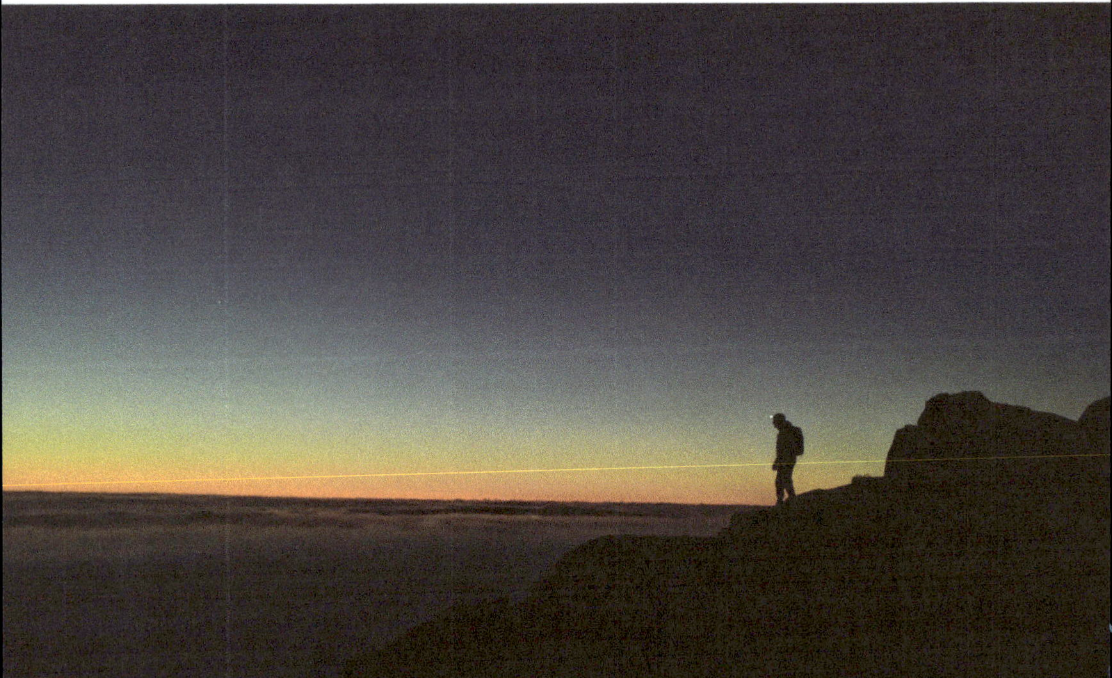

Honeycomb Tiffin

This cake is one of the biggest hits with my mountaineering friends. Best made in the cooler months of the year, as it's prone to getting a bit melty on warm summer days. There is a lot of fun to be had making your own honeycomb, but it's not essential, you can use a little cheat instead, making this one of the quickest no-bake recipes for the hills. What's more, it's absolutely delicious and a great alternative for those who, like me, think raisins in chocolate are a bit weird ...

Ingredients

110g butter

200g milk chocolate

40g dark chocolate

3 tbsp golden syrup

250g digestive biscuits, broken into small pieces

(ginger also works well)

Honeycomb to sprinkle (the recipe below will give you far more than you need, alternatively you can use a couple of Crunchie bars broken into pieces)

Method

1. Line a 20 x 20cm tin with baking parchment.

2. Place the butter, milk chocolate and golden syrup in a glass bowl over a pan of simmering water, stirring occasionally until everything has melted.

3. Take the bowl off the heat, being careful of the steam, and stir in the digestive biscuits.

4. Pour the mixture into the lined tin and press down with the back of a spoon.

5. Melt the dark chocolate in the glass bowl (no need to rinse the bowl first) over the pan of simmering water. Meanwhile, sprinkle over the pieces of honeycomb and press into the mixture.

6. Drizzle over the dark chocolate and then refrigerate for a couple of hours until completely set before removing from the tin and cutting into squares.

Homemade
Honeycomb

7. Grease a large roasting tin with sunflower oil and line
    with baking parchment.

8. In a large pan, place 200g caster sugar, 100g clear
    honey and 4 tbsp water over a low heat until the sugar
    has dissolved.

9. Add a sugar thermometer and bring to the boil over
    a high heat until the mixture reaches 150C on the
    thermometer.

10. As soon as it does, take immediately off the heat and
    quickly whisk in 1 tbsp bicarbonate of soda with a
    balloon whisk.

11. The mixture will froth up alarmingly, but don't worry! This
    is meant to happen. Pour straight into the prepared tin
    and leave to completely set before you turn it out and
    break it into pieces.

NOTE: Take extra care when handling sugar at high
temperatures.

Fruit Scones

One of my mum's favourite pastimes was running a small cake stall at agricultural shows, and the one thing she never went without was a glut of freshly baked scones. On the bottom of the handwritten recipe she gave me was "don't put a rolling pin anywhere near them". There was a second comment about the type of fruit to use, but it's best I don't include that here owing to the colourful language she used ...

They're very light and fluffy, best served fresh, but likewise they taste great for a day or so after. I love experimenting with a variety of flavoured curds. Simply slice and add your favourite topping, sandwich back together, and wrap in tinfoil to add to your rucksack.

Ingredients

450g self-raising flour
110g butter
110g sultanas
50g caster sugar
140ml milk

Method

1. Preheat the oven to 200C fan. Line two baking sheets.

2. Rub the flour and butter together until it resembles super-fine breadcrumbs. Stir in the sugar and fruit.

3. Add the milk and stir together with a round-bladed knife, finally bringing the mixture together with your hands.

4. Turn out onto a lightly floured surface and press down gently with the palm of your hand until the dough is approximately 2.5cm thick.

5. Cut out rounds with a circular cutter. You can use any size depending on your preference. I like to make them small so I can eat two! Reroll as necessary.

6. Place on the lined baking trays well-spaced apart and bake in the oven for 15 minutes.

7. Eat as soon as they are cool enough to handle. Store any left over in an airtight container, or wrap in foil for the hills.

Mini Cinnamon Swirls

These are an amazingly quick and simple treat, great for picnics, breakfast, mid-morning coffee snacks or any other time you fancy a little nugget of indulgence.

I make mini ones in a twelve-hole muffin tin. Be sure to grease the tin well and they won't stick.

Ingredients

320g ready-rolled sheet of shop-bought puff pastry (refrigerated or defrosted from frozen as per packet instructions)

2 tbsp butter

2 tbsp light soft brown sugar

Handful of sultanas or raisins, plus any other leftover dried fruit you have, such as candied peel and cranberries

2 tsp cinnamon

Method

1. Preheat the oven to 180C fan. Grease a twelve-hole muffin tin.

2. Unroll your puff pastry sheet flat on a lightly floured worktop.

3. Melt the butter in a small pan over a very low heat until just melted.

4. Spread the butter all over your pastry sheet with a pastry brush, then evenly sprinkle the sugar, dried fruit and cinnamon over the top.

5. Roll the pastry carefully along the long edge, tucking in any stray fruit as you go, so you end up with a long sausage-shaped log.

6. Cut in half, then cut each piece in half again. Finally cut each piece into three, so you have twelve pieces in total.

7. Place each piece in a separate hole in the muffin tin so that the swirl pattern faces upwards.

8. Bake for 15 minutes until golden brown.

9. Serve warm with a dusting of icing sugar.

Honey Cake

I absolutely adore honey, and this lightly-spiced cake is a real favourite. It's quite a solid sponge, so it travels well and is great for eating on the go. Just cut into really big chunks and wrap in greaseproof paper or stash in a tin. At home, serve warm with clotted cream or custard.

Ingredients

250g clear honey, plus 2 tbsp extra to glaze

225g butter

100g dark muscovado sugar

3 large eggs

300g self-raising flour

2 tsp mixed spice

Method

1. Preheat the oven to 140 fan. Grease and line a 20cm square cake tin.

2. Put the butter, honey and sugar in a medium pan and melt slowly over a low heat. Once everything has melted together turn the heat up and boil for one minute. Take off the heat and leave to cool.

3. Beat the eggs together in a large bowl. Add the flour, spice and honey mixture and beat again until smooth and runny.

4. Pour the mixture into the lined tin and bake for around 1 hour, checking every five minutes after 50 minutes, until a skewer inserted into the centre of the cake comes out clean.

5. Remove from the oven and brush over the extra honey to create a lovely sticky glaze.

6. Once completely cold store in an airtight container.

Salted Caramel Shortbread

Ingredients

For the shortbread:

80g semolina

150g butter

80g golden caster sugar

150g plain flour

For the caramel:

185g butter

75g caster sugar

3 tbsp golden syrup

397g tin condensed milk

1 tsp salt

150g milk or dark chocolate for the topping

Method

1. Preheat the oven to 160C. Line a 17.5 x 27.5cm deep rectangle tin with baking parchment.

2. Rub together the ingredients for the shortbread in a mixing bowl and press down into your lined baking tin. Bake for 20-25 minutes until just turning golden brown, then remove from the oven and leave to cool.

3. Whilst the shortbread cools, make the caramel. Place all the ingredients into a large heavy-based saucepan and melt everything over a low heat. Once the sugar has dissolved, turn the heat up a little until the mixture begins to boil. Stir constantly whilst boiling for around 5 minutes, until the caramel turns dark in colour and thickens. Add the teaspoon of salt, then pour over your biscuit base and leave to set.

4. Melt the chocolate in a bowl over a pan of simmering water, then spread evenly over the top of your caramel. Once set, cut into bars.

Savoury Bakes

Chorizo filled Sausage Rolls

Everything tastes good with chorizo, and these sausage rolls are no exception. They're super easy to make if you're using shop-bought pastry, and cook in under 30 minutes. They're fabulous straight out of the oven, but also good cold, wrapped up for a picnic or fellside sustenance.

Ingredients

375g puff pastry, defrosted

Plain flour for dusting

2 large Maris Piper potatoes cut into small pieces

225g chorizo

Small bunch of parsley, roughly chopped

2 tbsp nigella seeds

1 egg, beaten

Method

1. Roll out the pastry onto a lightly floured worktop to approximately 32 x 20cm. Cut in half so you have two rectangles 32 x 10cm and place on a baking sheet in the fridge.

2. Meanwhile, boil the potatoes in water with a pinch of salt for 6 minutes. Drain and leave to cool.

3. Remove the chorizo skin and place the meat into a food processor with the parsley, 1 tbsp nigella seeds and the potatoes and pulse everything together until just combined, but don't overdo it. You want everything to be mushed together but not puréed.

4. Heat the oven to 180C fan.

5. Remove the pastry from the fridge and shape the chorizo along the length of the pastry in a sausage shape. Brush the edges of the pastry with some of the egg and roll, tucking the meat and potato sausage into the centre as you do so, overlapping the two edges of pastry, until you have the seam tucked underneath.

6. Cut the rolls into 8 pieces each and place on lined baking sheets. Brush with the remaining egg and scatter with the nigella seeds.

7. Bake for 25-30 minutes until golden.

Pork Pies

Pork pies can be a real faff to make, but boy are they worth it. I make these with my son as he loves them so much – a real pork pie fiend. Don't be scared of the hot water crust pastry, it's really easy to do and you can patch up the bases in the muffin tin easily enough if you have any tears. I don't tend to fill mine with jelly, but if you want to you can soften a large sheet of gelatine in cold water for a few minutes, then dissolve it in 200ml boiling chicken stock, and dribble it into the holes on top of the pies as soon as they come out of the oven.

Ingredients

For the filling:

1 onion, finely chopped

360g pork loin, finely chopped

110g bacon, finely chopped

½ tsp allspice

Salt and pepper to season

Small bunch of flat leaf parsley, leaves only, finely chopped

For the pastry:

270g plain flour

60g strong white bread flour

60g butter

70g lard

1 tsp salt

140ml boiling water

1 egg

Method

1. Preheat the oven to 170C fan. You will need a 12-hole muffin tin.

2. To make the filling, mix the onion, pork, bacon and parsley into a bowl and season well.

3. For the hot water crust pastry, put both flours into a bowl and rub in the butter.

4. Melt the lard in a small pan over a low heat. Add the boiling water and salt.

5. Pour the liquid into the flour and mix with a spoon to bring it all together.

6. As soon as it is cool enough to handle, tip the dough mixture onto a lightly floured surface and bring together into a ball.

7. Roll out the pastry to around 3mm thick. Work as quickly as you can before the pastry becomes too cold and brittle.

8. Using a large cutter, cut out 12 circles to line the bottom of the muffin tin holes. The pastry should come all the way up the sides and stand proud slightly. Then using a smaller cutter cut out 12 lids the size of the muffin tin holes. Reroll the pastry if you need to.

9. Fill each pastry case with the filling, and place the lids on top. Crimp the bases and lids together by pressing gently with a fork to seal, then using a skewer make a small hole in the top of each to let out the hot air whilst baking.

10. Finally, brush the top of each pie with beaten egg.

11. Bake in the oven for 50 minutes until golden brown.

Quiche

I've amalgamated a number of recipes to create this quiche as I liked something about all of them and could never decide which was my favourite. I generally bake this in a round flan dish, but you can just as easily bake it in a similar volume rectangular tray if you want to cut it into square pieces. Nothing beats homemade pastry, so if you want to make your own I've included a recipe on the following page, or you can use shop-bought which I have demonstrated for this recipe.

Ingredients

320g pre-rolled shortcrust pastry sheet (chilled)

170g bacon lardons

½ large or 1 small onion chopped

150g gruyere cheese (or alternative)

200ml whole milk

3 medium eggs (large are fine too)

Pinch of ground nutmeg

Ground black pepper

6 cherry tomatoes

Basil to serve (optional)

Method

1. Preheat the oven to 180C fan. Line a 30cm flan dish with the pastry and carefully press it down into the corners and over the edge of the top of the dish, cutting away any excess with a knife. I always use a glass Pyrex dish and never need to grease first.

2. Prick all over with a fork, then line the pastry with baking parchment and pour in baking beans if you have some. Bake for 15 minutes, then remove the parchment and baking beans and bake for a further 5 minutes.

3. Whilst the pastry bakes, fry the bacon lardons and onion in a small frying pan for around 5 minutes, until the onion is soft and the bacon is just browning but not crispy.

4. Grate the cheese into a bowl, saving some to sprinkle later, add the milk, eggs, nutmeg and pepper. You shouldn't need any additional salt with the bacon and cheese already being quite salty.

5. Pour into the baked flan case. Add halved cherry tomatoes to the surface facing up, sprinkle over the reserved cheese, turn the oven down to 160C fan and bake for 25 - 30 minutes until golden brown.

6. Leave to rest for 5 minutes before slicing. Sprinkle with basil leaves if you have any and serve warm or cold.

Tuna Fish Flan

This final recipe is another of my mum's staples when we were growing up. It's super simple, deliciously tasty, and was always popular with our whole family. It's great served hot or cold, and if you keep pastry in the freezer, cans of tuna in the cupboard, and a few eggs in the fridge, you can make it any time you're short.

Ingredients

For the pastry:

175g plain flour

100g salted butter

1 egg yolk

For the filling:

4 x 125g tins of tuna, either in sunflower oil or spring water

4 eggs

100ml whole milk

Freshly ground black pepper to taste

Method

1. First, make the pastry. Measure the flour and butter into a bowl and rub flour into the butter with your fingertips until the mixture starts to come together. Add the egg yolk and 4tsp of cold water and bring into a ball. Wrap and fridge for 30 minutes.

2. Once the pastry has chilled, preheat the oven to 180C fan. Roll out the pastry on a lightly-floured work surface until it is big enough to line your flan dish bottom and up the sides.

3. With the help of your rolling pin, drape the pastry over the dish and carefully press it down and into the corners and over the edge of the top of the dish, cutting away any excess with a knife.

4. Prick all over with a fork, then line the pastry with baking parchment and pour in baking beans if you have some. Bake for 15 minutes, then remove the parchment and baking beans and bake for a further 5 minutes.

5. Whilst the pastry bakes, mix all the filling ingredients together in a bowl, then pour into the baked case.

6. Turn the oven down to 160C fan and put the flan back in the oven for a further 35 - 40 minutes until starting to brown.

www.ingramcontent.com/pod-product-compliance
Lightning Source LLC
Chambersburg PA
CBHW050751150626
46551CB00039BA/2129